A Guide to
AMERICAN STATES
★ ★ ★ ★ ★

Maryland

THE OLD LINE STATE

MEDIA ENHANCED BOOKS

AV2
BY WEIGL

ADDED VALUE • AUDIO VISUAL

www.av2books.com

AV² provides enriched content that supplements and complements this book. Weigl's AV² books strive to create inspired learning and engage young minds in a total learning experience.

Your AV² Media Enhanced books come alive with...

 Audio
Listen to sections of the book read aloud.

 Key Words
Study vocabulary, and complete a matching word activity.

 Video
Watch informative video clips.

 Quizzes
Test your knowledge.

Go to **www.av2books.com**, and enter this book's unique code.

 Embedded Weblinks
Gain additional information for research.

Slide Show
View images and captions, and prepare a presentation.

BOOK CODE

P 6 9 6 5 2 2

 Try This!
Complete activities and hands-on experiments.

... and much, much more!

AV² by Weigl brings you media enhanced books that support active learning.

Published by AV² by Weigl
350 5th Avenue, 59th Floor
New York, NY 10118
Website: www.av2books.com   www.weigl.com

Library of Congress Cataloging-in-Publication Data

Craats, Rennay.
 Maryland / Rennay Craats.
   p. cm. -- (A guide to American states)
 Includes index.
 ISBN 978-1-61690-792-1 (hardcover : alk. paper) -- ISBN 978-1-61690-468-5 (online)
 1. Maryland--Juvenile literature. I. Title.
 F181.3.C735 2011
 975.2--dc23
                        2011018332

Printed in the United States of America in North Mankato, Minnesota

052011
WEP180511

Project Coordinator Jordan McGill
Art Director Terry Paulhus

Photo Credits
Every reasonable effort has been made to trace ownership and to obtain permission to reprint copyright material. The publishers would be pleased to have any errors or omissions brought to their attention so that they may be corrected in subsequent printings.

Weigl acknowledges Getty Images as its primary image supplier for this title.

Contents

Racing with sail-powered Chesapeake Bay log canoes is an Eastern Shore tradition.

Introduction

Maryland is sometimes called "America in Miniature," a nickname reflecting both its small size and its great **diversity**. Although it covers a land area of only 9,774 square miles and is the ninth-smallest state of the United States, Maryland contains a great variety of landscapes and lifestyles.

Baltimore is Maryland's largest city and has one of the busiest ports in the country. This leading industrial center lies at the head of the Patapsco River **estuary**, 15 miles above Chesapeake Bay, which divides the state into two regions, the Eastern Shore and the Western Shore. Baltimore is a popular tourist destination and contains many historic sites.

Shops on Thames Street, near Baltimore's waterfront, show the colorful brickwork that is common throughout the city.

The National Aquarium in Baltimore displays 16,500 examples of 660 different species.

Marylanders fought hard to achieve independence for themselves and for the United States. On April 28, 1788, Maryland achieved statehood, becoming the seventh of the original 13 colonies to join the Union. Its citizens welcomed this new freedom and the new government. In 1790, George Washington, as the first U.S. president, chose the District of Columbia, to be built on land donated by Maryland and neighboring Virginia, as the new capital of the United States.

In the 20th and early 21st centuries, Maryland's population soared, from about 1.2 million in 1900 to more than 5.7 million in 2010. High-tech industries grew, and computers, scientific research, and aerospace became important sectors of the state's economy.

Where Is Maryland?

Maryland is located on the Atlantic coast and is part of the Middle Atlantic region of the United States. Maryland is bordered to the north by Pennsylvania, to the east by Delaware and the Atlantic Ocean, and to the west by West Virginia. To the south and west, the Potomac River forms part of the border that separates Maryland from West Virginia and Virginia. On the Maryland side of the Potomac, and surrounded by Maryland on three sides, is the District of Columbia, or Washington, D.C.

The history of White's Ferry service dates back to the early 1800s. The ferry travels along a cable that connects it to the Maryland and Virginia shores.

The two spans that make up the Chesapeake Bay Bridge use a combined total of more than 126,000 tons of steel and 286,000 cubic yards of concrete.

Access to Maryland is made easy by the roughly 31,000 miles of highways that cross the state. Interstate 95 connects the state to Washington, D.C., in the south and to Philadelphia in the north. The state's biggest air terminal is Baltimore-Washington International Airport, also known as Thurgood Marshall Airport. This airport serves the Washington, D.C., area and provides service to most domestic and many foreign destinations.

For a scenic voyage to Virginia, travelers can board White's Ferry. This car ferry is the only one that regularly crosses the Potomac River. It connects Montgomery County in Maryland to Loudoun County in Virginia.

Maryland measures about 250 miles from east to west and 90 miles from north to south, but its shape is very uneven. At its narrowest point, the state is less than 2 miles wide from north to south.

Most transportation routes in Maryland run through Baltimore. The Baltimore Harbor Tunnel and Fort McHenry Tunnel carry automobile traffic beneath the city's harbor.

Two airports in northern Virginia serve Maryland as well. Both Dulles International Airport and Reagan National Airport provide passenger and freight access to the state.

The Chesapeake Bay Bridge opened in 1952. The 4.3-mile bridge links Maryland's Eastern and Western shores.

The country's first federal highway, the Cumberland Road, ran from Cumberland, Maryland, to Vandalia, Illinois. It was built between 1811 and 1837.

Mapping Maryland

Maryland has a total area of 12,407 square miles, including 9,774 square miles of land and 2,633 square miles of water. About 70 percent of Maryland's water area lies along the coast, while the remainder is inland. Despite its small size, the state has nearly 3,200 miles of shoreline.

Sites and Symbols

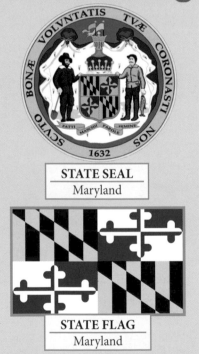

STATE SEAL
Maryland

STATE BIRD
Baltimore Oriole

STATE FLOWER
Black-eyed Susan

STATE FLAG
Maryland

STATE DOG
Chesapeake Bay Retriever

STATE TREE
White Oak

Nickname The Old Line State

Motto *Fatti Maschii Parole Femine* (Strong Deeds, Gentle Words)

Song "Maryland, My Maryland," words by James Ryder Randall and sung to the tune of "O, Tannenbaum"

Entered the Union April 28, 1788, as the 7th state

Capital Annapolis

Population (2010 Census) 5,773,552 Ranked 19th state

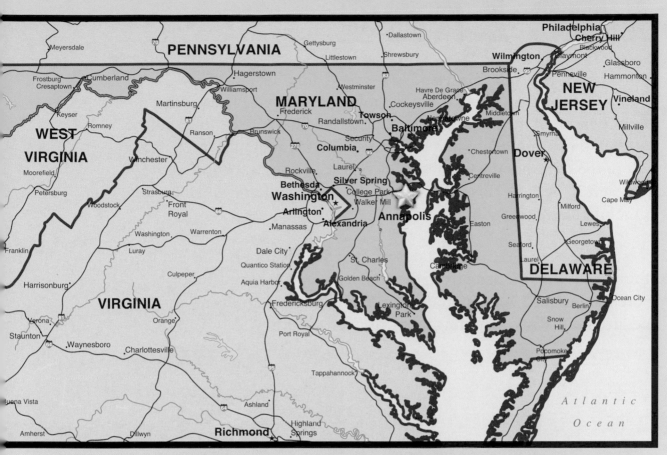

STATE CAPITAL

Annapolis, the state capital, is not only the center of state government but also the home of the U.S. Naval Academy. Located about 25 miles south of Baltimore, Annapolis was named in honor of Princess Anne, who ruled Britain as Queen Anne in the early 1700s. The city has been the capital of Maryland since 1695 and has a population of about 37,000.

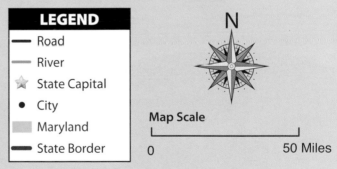

LEGEND

——	Road
——	River
★	State Capital
●	City
▨	Maryland
━━	State Border

Map Scale

0   50 Miles

N

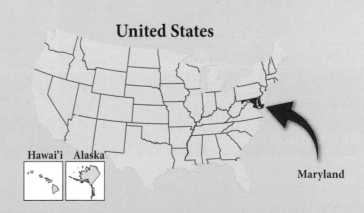

United States

Hawai'i   Alaska

Maryland

The Land

From east to west, Maryland has several different landscapes. A coastal plain merges into the rolling Piedmont Plateau. To the west of the plateau is a section of the Blue Ridge Mountains. Between those mountains and the Appalachian Mountains, in the far west of the state, lies the Cumberland Valley. The highest point in the state, at 3,360 feet, is Hoye Crest on Backbone Mountain, which is part of the Appalachian chain.

Chesapeake Bay is one of the state's most notable features. This body of water juts into the state from the south, giving Maryland a long shoreline. About 2,700 different species of plants and animals live in and around the bay, including many fish and waterfowl.

BLUE RIDGE MOUNTAINS

The Blue Ridge Mountains slice through western Frederick County, in the northern part of the state.

CHESAPEAKE BAY

More than one-third of the nation's annual blue-crab catch comes from Chesapeake Bay.

I DIDN'T KNOW THAT!

Maryland takes its name from Britain's Queen Henrietta Maria, wife of King Charles I. In 1632 she signed the charter that founded the colony.

Francis Scott Key wrote "The Star-Spangled Banner" in September 1814. The U.S. Congress made it the official national anthem in 1931.

Maryland's state flag honors two families that were important in the early history of the state, the Calverts and the Crosslands. The black and yellow design on the flag represents the Calvert family crest, and the red and white shield represents the Crossland family crest.

St. Mary's City was the first capital of Maryland. In 1695 the capital was moved to Annapolis.

U.S. presidents use Camp David for meetings with foreign officials and for rest and relaxation. The presidential retreat in Maryland's Catoctin Mountains was created in 1942.

CAMP DAVID

ASSATEAGUE

Assateague National Wildlife Refuge supports a population of more than 300 wild horses.

POTOMAC RIVER

The Potomac River defines the border between Maryland and Virginia and drains more than 3,800 square miles of Maryland territory.

The record snowfall during the winter of 2009–2010 was four times the annual average for the Baltimore area.

Climate

Maryland's climate is hot and humid in the summer, with an average summer temperature of 74° Fahrenheit. Winters in Maryland are usually mild, with an average temperature of about 35° F. Most of the precipitation in Maryland falls as rain, but snow is common in winter. From December 2009 through February 2010, more than 80 inches of snow fell at Baltimore-Washington International Airport, a new record.

The highest temperature ever recorded in Maryland was 109° F on several dates in different locations. The lowest temperature ever recorded in Maryland was –40° F, at Oakland, on January 13, 1912.

Average Annual Precipitation Across Maryland

Hagerstown usually gets less annual precipitation than most other places in Maryland. What factors might account for the difference?

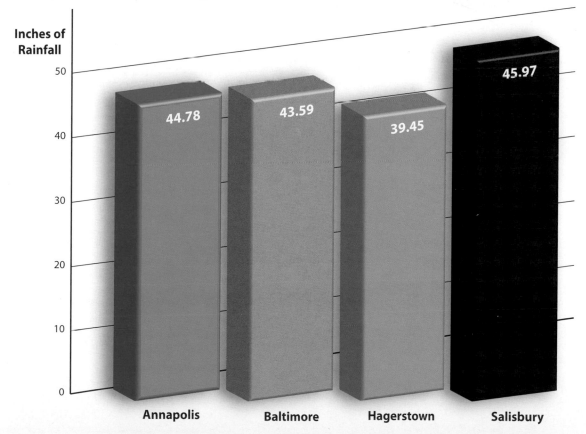

Inches of Rainfall

- Annapolis — 44.78
- Baltimore — 43.59
- Hagerstown — 39.45
- Salisbury — 45.97

Natural Resources

Important reserves of coal are found in Maryland's mountains. Miners dig most of the coal out of large pits called strip mines. Maryland produces more than 2 million tons of coal each year. Elsewhere in the state, limestone, sandstone, marble, granite, sand, and gravel are mined. The construction industry uses these resources as building stone and to make roads.

Coal mines supply fuel for power plants that produce more than one-half of Maryland's electricity.

Workers at "fish lifts" near the Conowingo Dam help to preserve Maryland's shad population. The lifts transport the fish to their Susquehanna River spawning grounds.

Water is another important natural resource in Maryland. The boundary between the upland plateau and the coastal plain is called the fall line. Where rivers cross the fall line, waterfalls occur. Energy from the falling water is harnessed to produce **hydroelectric** power. The Conowingo Dam serves both as a large hydroelectric power plant and as a bridge across the Susquehanna River.

I DIDN'T KNOW THAT!

Chesapeake Bay is the largest estuary anywhere in North America.

Most of Maryland's electricity comes from plants fueled by coal or oil.

Two nuclear power plants, located in Lusby, provide more than one-fourth of the electricity generated in the state.

The Conowingo Dam is more than 4,000 feet long and 100 feet high. It was completed in 1928 and expanded in 1978.

Maryland contains more than 250,000 acres of state parks and recreation areas.

Fisheries began booming in the 1800s. Chesapeake Bay was filled with fish, clams, crabs, and oysters. Crisfield was the oyster capital of the state.

"Oyster wars" raged in the 1800s as Maryland and Virginia fishers began to raid each other's oyster beds. Some of these disputes escalated into violent gunfights.

Plants

Maryland has kept its beautiful forests largely intact. More than two-fifths of the state's land area is covered with forests, and more than half of the forested area has hardwood trees such as oaks and hickories. Black locust, black cherry, and ash trees are also common in the state. The dominant softwood tree is the loblolly pine.

Sweet gum and bald cypress trees flourish in the **wetlands** in the south. The wetlands, which cover about 600,000 acres, are home to thousands of other plants and animals. To the west, hemlock and white pine trees grow in the mountains.

CYPRESS TREES

Battle Creek Cypress Swamp is a 100-acre nature sanctuary in Calvert County.

WHITE OAK

A mature white oak may produce up to 10,000 acorns annually.

LOBLOLLY PINES

The loblolly pine typically stands between 90 and 110 feet tall but may reach heights of 150 feet or more.

SWEET GUM

The sweet gum tree produces spiky "gumballs" that turn from green to brown. They are more than an inch across.

Maryland has about 50 state parks and forests.

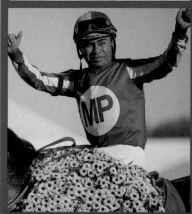

The black-eyed Susan was adopted as Maryland's state flower in 1918. This bright yellow flower blooms in late summer. By tradition, the winner of the Preakness horse race gets a blanket of black-eyed Susans.

The white oak became the official state tree in 1941.

The Chesapeake Bay retriever became the official state dog in 1964. The breed originated in the state in the early 1800s. Maryland also has an official state cat. It is the calico cat, which has orange, black, and white fur.

The Free State is a nickname often applied to Maryland. The state received this nickname in 1923 from Hamilton Owens, the editor of the *Baltimore Sun* newspaper.

Animals

The forests are home to many different kinds of wildlife. Animals found in Maryland include white-tailed deer, black bears, wild turkeys, bald eagles, and orioles. The Delmarva fox squirrel, an **endangered species**, lives near Chesapeake Bay. Over development and competition for food have caused a decline in the number of these animals. They are found in wooded parts of Virginia and Maryland.

The Baltimore oriole, the official state bird, inhabits Maryland's forests. The orange and black of the male's feathers are similar to the colors on the Calvert family crest. The bird takes its name from George Calvert, who was known as Lord Baltimore.

Hikers need to keep their eyes to the ground, as the state is home to some 27 species of snakes. Snakes found in the state include the green, corn, yellow rat, milk, king, and garter. Several species, including the northern copperhead and timber rattlesnake, pose a danger because of their venom.

BALD EAGLE

The Chesapeake Bay Environmental Center takes care of injured or orphaned bald eagles until they can released into the wild.

WILD TURKEYS

A recent survey counted about 5,000 wild turkeys in Maryland.

NORTHERN COPPERHEAD

Rarely more than 3 feet long, the northern copperhead lives mostly in rocky, wooded areas of the state.

BLACK BEAR

The black bear was nearly extinct in Maryland in the mid-1960s. Today, hundreds of black bears roam Maryland's westernmost counties.

The Delmarva fox squirrel is named after the Delmarva Peninsula, where it is found.

The peregrine falcon can be found in the skies near cliffs and bluffs along Maryland's coast. These master hunters can reach speeds of 200 miles per hour as they dive for food.

Bald eagles, robins, blue jays, cardinals, wrens, and mockingbirds are among the more than 400 species of birds that fly in Maryland's skies.

Tourism

More than 20 million people visit Maryland every year. Many tourists travel to Ocean City, the state's main seaside resort. South of Ocean City in the Atlantic Ocean lies Assateague Island National Seashore. This nearly 40-mile-long island is home to herds of wild horses.

Fort McHenry National Monument is one of Maryland's major historic attractions. Here, in 1814, while watching the British attack the fort, Francis Scott Key wrote a poem called "The Star-Spangled Banner," which later became the country's official national anthem. Another important attraction is Antietam National Battlefield, the site of a bloody Civil War battle. About 23,000 soldiers were killed or wounded at Antietam.

OCEAN CITY

Ocean City was a sleepy fishing village until the 1870s, when the coming of the railroad transformed it into a bustling resort town.

NATIONAL AQUARIUM

The daily dolphin show is a main attraction at Baltimore's National Aquarium, which receives visits from about 1.6 million people each year.

FORT McHENRY

Designed by a French engineer in 1798, Fort McHenry was built to defend the port of Baltimore.

ANNAPOLIS

Graduation ceremonies at the U.S. Naval Academy in Annapolis feature a jet flyover by members of the Blue Angels.

Crownsville hosts the Maryland Renaissance Festival every year from August to October.

Tourists spend about $9 billion in Maryland every year.

More American soldiers were killed and wounded at the Battle of Antietam than died in the American Revolution, the War of 1812, the Mexican-American War, and the Spanish-American War combined.

St. Mary's City is home to an 800-acre living history museum. The museum contains re-creations of a tobacco **plantation**, the state house, and one of the first ships that took settlers to the state.

Visitors come to Annapolis to tour the U.S. Naval Academy and the Maryland State House.

Industry

I n the 20th century, manufacturing became a leading industry in Maryland. Major manufactured products in the state include electric and electronic equipment, food and food products, instruments, chemicals, industrial machinery, and transportation equipment. Printing and publishing and the high-tech sector, including aerospace and biotechnology, are also important to the state's economy.

Industries in Maryland
Value of Goods and Services in Millions of Dollars

Government accounts for about 18 percent of Maryland's economy. This is a higher percentage than in many other states. What reasons might account for the difference?

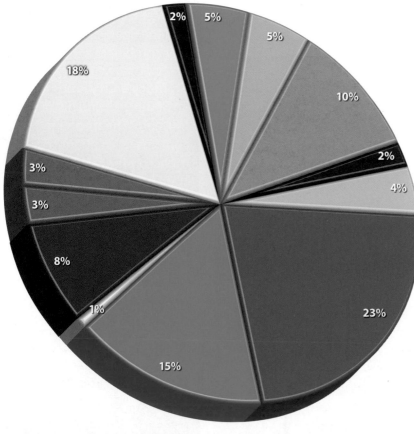

LEGEND

✱ Agriculture, Forestry, and Fishing	$730
✱ Mining	$123
■ Utilities	$6,033
■ Construction	$14,143
■ Manufacturing	$15,186
■ Wholesale and Retail Trade	$29,096
■ Transportation	$5,397
■ Media and Entertainment	$12,549
■ Finance, Insurance, and Real Estate	$66,115
■ Professional and Technical Services	$43,355
■ Education	$3,983
■ Health Care	$22,087
■ Hotels and Restaurants	$7,846
■ Other Services	$7,721
■ Government	$52,433

TOTAL **$286,797**

*Less than 1%. Percentages may not add to 100 because of rounding.

One of Maryland's leading manufacturing companies is Black & Decker, based in Towson. Black & Decker is a worldwide manufacturer of power tools, hardware, and other home-improvement products. The company supplies products and services to more than 100 countries, and it manufactures products in about a dozen countries.

Founded as a small machine shop in Baltimore in 1910, Black & Decker opened its first large factory in Towson in 1917.

Much of Maryland's manufacturing takes place in Baltimore and the surrounding area.

The Baltimore and Ohio Railroad was founded in Baltimore in 1827. It was the first steam railway chartered in the United States.

Black & Decker built the drill that NASA astronauts used to remove core samples from the Moon.

Lockheed Martin, a leading aerospace company, has its headquarters in Maryland.

More than 110,000 people in Maryland are employed in the state's manufacturing industry.

About one in five Marylanders works for a local, state, or federal government agency.

Goods and Services

Maryland's coastal location makes it a prime center for seafood. Crisfield, on the tip of the Eastern Shore, is nicknamed the Seafood Capital of the World. Maryland is the country's top provider of crabs as well as several kinds of fish. Oysters are still an important seafood catch, but pollution and disease have harmed the oyster beds. In the late 20th century, scientists began efforts to restore oyster beds in Chesapeake Bay.

Farms cover nearly two-fifths of the state's land. Flowers and other **nursery products**, corn, soybeans, and tobacco are particularly important crops. Vegetables are grown and processed on the Eastern Shore. Barley, oats, wheat, and hay are also valuable.

Maryland's restaurants are renowned for their crabcakes and grilled or fried soft-shell crabs.

Scientists at John Hopkins University have pioneered in understanding, treating, and curing cancer.

Livestock and livestock products account for about two-thirds of Maryland's farm income. The state is an important producer of **broiler chickens**, which account for more than half of the income from livestock. Maryland farmers also raise cows, hogs, and turkeys.

The service sector, which includes many industries, employs about four-fifths of the state's workers. Many service employees live in Maryland and commute to work in and around Washington, D.C. These employees include federal government workers and military personnel. Among the major institutions that employ Marylanders are the National Institutes of Health, the National Naval Medical Center, the Smithsonian Institution, and the Goddard Space Flight Center.

Maryland has one of the best-educated workforces in the country. More than 15 percent of all Marylanders have a graduate or professional degree. The University of Maryland is the main state-sponsored institution for higher learning. It has its main campus at College Park and other branches in Baltimore and Princess Anne. One of the state's outstanding private higher education and research institutions is Johns Hopkins University in Baltimore.

American Indians

Early peoples hunted in the Maryland area at least 10,000 years ago. By the year 800, American Indians in Maryland had begun raising crops and hunting with bows and arrows. They established permanent villages by about 1200. Most of the Indians in the Maryland region belonged to groups speaking a language in the Algonquian language family. An Iroquoian-speaking group, the Susquehanna, lived along the Susquehanna River.

Father Andrew White, an English missionary, traveled among the Piscataway Indians and learned their language in the mid-1600s.

American Indians in Maryland hunted deer and other animals, fished the waterways, and grew tobacco, corn, and squash. They also traded blankets and food with other Indian groups in places that are now in Ohio and New York. As Europeans began to settle in the region, most of the Indians moved westward. Those who stayed often fought with the settlers over land. They also died from new diseases brought by the Europeans.

The Susquehanna Indians were skilled hunters and warriors.

About 3,000 years ago there were some 8,000 American Indians living in the Maryland area. Scholars have found evidence that Indians during this period made pottery and relied on oysters as a food source.

The Iroquois and Algonquian-speaking groups often fought one another. The Iroquois killed many Indians from other groups in fighting along Chesapeake Bay.

The Potomac, Piscataway, Accokeek, and Choptank were among the 40 different American Indian groups that lived in Maryland.

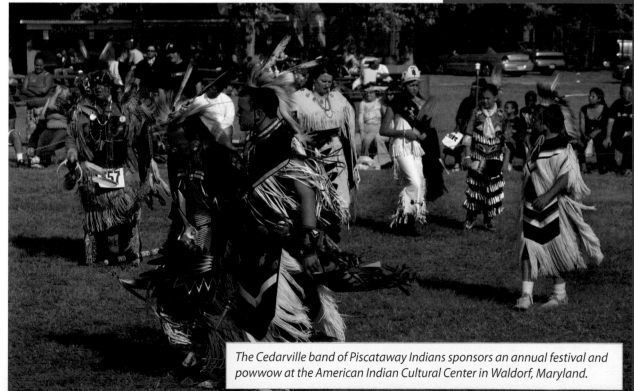

The Cedarville band of Piscataway Indians sponsors an annual festival and powwow at the American Indian Cultural Center in Waldorf, Maryland.

Maryland's name honors Queen Henrietta Maria. A Frenchwoman, she married King Charles I of England in 1625.

Explorers

A lthough some historians think that the Vikings reached Chesapeake Bay, most believe that Giovanni da Verrazzano was the first European in what is now Maryland. He sailed through the bay in 1524 but did not land in the area. Captain John Smith, an English explorer and a leader of the Jamestown settlement in Virginia, was the first European to map the area, in 1608. At this time, explorers from England were reaching North America and claiming the shores for their king. The land they claimed included much of Maryland's coast, including Chesapeake Bay. In 1632, King Charles I promised part of the Chesapeake Bay area to George Calvert, or Lord Baltimore, and named the area Maryland in honor of the queen, Henrietta Maria.

Lord Baltimore began planning an American colony for Roman Catholics who wished to escape **persecution** by Protestants in Britain. Lord Baltimore died before reaching his goal, but his son Cecilius took over. He sent his brother Leonard to North America with about 140 settlers in November 1633.

Timeline of Settlement

Early Exploration

1524 Giovanni da Verrazzano sails through Chesapeake Bay.

1608 Captain John Smith explores and maps the Chesapeake Bay region.

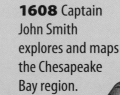

First Colonies Established

1632 George Calvert, or Lord Baltimore, applies for a charter for the Maryland colony.

1632 After Lord Baltimore's death, his son Cecilius Calvert receives the Maryland charter.

1634 Settlers found St. Mary's City, which becomes the first capital of Maryland.

Further Settlement

1649 Maryland enacts the first law in the American colonies guaranteeing religious freedom for all Christians. Protestants found the town of Providence, later renamed Annapolis.

1695 Annapolis replaces St. Mary's City as the capital of Maryland.

1729 Baltimore is founded near a port that is used for shipping tobacco grown in Maryland.

American Revolution and Civil War

1776 Maryland joins other colonies in declaring independence from Britain. Troops from the Maryland Line fight bravely, earning praise from George Washington.

1788 Maryland ratifies the new U.S. Constitution and becomes the 7th state on April 28.

1861–1862 Although slavery is legal in the state, Maryland chooses not to join the Confederacy. The state becomes an important battleground in the early years of the Civil War.

Early Settlers

The charter from King Charles granted Cecilius, also known as Lord Baltimore, and his brother Leonard Calvert the land from the south shore of the Potomac River up to the 40th parallel, as well as most of the Delmarva Peninsula. Leonard and the settlers arrived in Maryland in 1634.

Map of Settlements and Resources in Early Maryland

4 *Tobacco growing became so important to the early economy of Maryland that settlers made tobacco leaves an official form of money in 1637.*

1 *Settlers from England founded St. Mary's City in 1634. It served as the capital of colonial Maryland until 1695.*

5 *The first European colonists fished with hook and line in the shallow waters of Chesapeake Bay. By the mid-1700s, commercial fishing for shad and herring had developed.*

6 *Colonists used timber from the Chesapeake region to build settlements and ships' masts.*

2 *Protestants founded a settlement named Providence in 1649. Later renamed Anne Arundel's Towne and then Annapolis, it has been the capital of Maryland since 1695.*

3 *Baltimore was a port before it was a town. Colonial lawmakers established the port of Baltimore in 1706 as a shipping center for Maryland-grown tobacco. As settlement along the Patapsco River expanded, the town of Baltimore was founded in 1729.*

N

Scale

0   50 Miles

LEGEND

Settlement	Wood
Tobacco	Maryland
River	State Border
Seafood	

At first, the settlers enjoyed good harvests and established strong ties with the American Indians in the area of St. Mary's City. The Indians traded furs and food for **textiles** and tools. They also helped the settlers grow corn. This assistance prevented the European newcomers from starving. The settlers also grew tobacco, which they sold to England. Using the money they made selling tobacco, the settlers established plantations to grow even more of the crop.

In the mid-1700s, Britain and France went to war for control of eastern North America. To pay for the war, Britain taxed settlers heavily on goods imported from Europe, including sugar, tea, and newspapers. This angered the settlers. In 1774, a year after the Boston Tea Party, colonists burned a ship loaded with tea at an Annapolis dock.

The high taxes led the colonists to stop buying from Britain and to fight for independence. By 1776 the American Revolution had swept across the colonies, and Marylanders took an active part. A group of soldiers called the Maryland Line joined the Continental Army. In 1776, four representatives from Maryland signed the Declaration of Independence.

St. Mary's City has a full-scale, operating replica of the Dove, one of the two ships that carried the first European settlers to Maryland in 1634.

I DIDN'T KNOW THAT!

Religious freedom for all Christians in Maryland came in 1649, with the passage of the first religious toleration act in the American colonies.

Baltimore native Charles Carroll was the only Roman Catholic to sign the Declaration of Independence.

The soldiers of the Maryland Line were known for their strength and bravery. They were rarely beaten in battle.

The most northerly of the Southern states, Maryland was a key battleground during the Civil War. With Virginia joining the Confederacy, the fate of the nation partly hinged on Maryland's decision to stay in or leave the Union. Maryland's Union loyalties ultimately saved Washington, D.C., from being surrendered to the Confederacy.

John Wilkes Booth was born near Bel Air. The actor assassinated President Abraham Lincoln at Ford's Theater in Washington, D.C., in 1865.

Notable People

Located on the dividing line between North and South, Maryland has been home to many leaders in the fight for equal rights. Others who have called Maryland their home include a pioneering congresswoman, an influential writer, exceptional athletes, and even a saint.

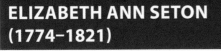

**ELIZABETH ANN SETON
(1774–1821)**

Elizabeth Ann Seton was the first native-born American to be named as a saint by the Catholic Church. She was born in New York City and became a Catholic in 1805. She devoted the rest of her life to teaching and helping the poor. In 1809 she founded a religious community, the Sisters of Charity, in Emmitsburg, Maryland, where she died in 1821. The Catholic Church declared her a saint in 1975.

**FREDERICK DOUGLASS
(1818–1895)**

Born to a slave woman on the Eastern Shore, Frederick Douglass grew up both in rural Maryland and in Baltimore. After he was treated cruelly by a slavemaster, he escaped to New York City in 1838. He spent the rest of his life speaking and writing against the evils of slavery. His most famous book was his *Narrative of the Life of Frederick Douglass, an American Slave, Written by Himself* (1845).

HARRIET TUBMAN (c. 1820–1913)

Harriet Tubman was born into slavery in Maryland's Dorchester County. She worked hard to end slavery, risking her life to help more than 300 slaves escape to freedom through the "Underground Railroad." During the Civil War, this brave woman worked as a nurse, a cook, and a spy.

THURGOOD MARSHALL (1908–1993)

Born in Baltimore, Thurgood Marshall graduated at the top of his class in law school. As a lawyer for the NAACP, he argued for equal rights for all Americans. He convinced the Supreme Court to outlaw the practice in many states of forcing black and white children to attend separate schools. In 1967, Marshall became the first African American to serve on the Supreme Court.

NANCY PELOSI (1940–)

Nancy Pelosi comes from one of Baltimore's leading political families. Her father and brother both served as mayor of Baltimore. Pelosi moved to California, where she won election to the U.S. House of Representatives. From 2007 through 2010 she was speaker of the House, the first woman ever to hold that high office.

I DIDN'T KNOW THAT!

Upton Sinclair (1878–1968) was born in Baltimore and became one of the most widely read writers of the early 1900s. His novel *The Jungle* exposed unfair and dangerous practices in Chicago's meat packing industry. His writings inspired laws that made the nation's food healthier and working conditions safer.

Michael Phelps (1985–) is a champion swimmer who developed his skills at the North Baltimore Aquatic Club. He won six gold and two bronze medals at the 2004 Summer Olympics in Athens, Greece. He did even better in 2008, winning a record-breaking eight gold medals at the Summer Olympics in Beijing, China.

Population

Maryland has quite a large population for such a small state. At the time of the 2010 Census, Maryland had a population of nearly 5.8 million people, making it the 19th most populous state in the country. Between 2000 and 2010, Maryland's population grew by 9 percent, slightly less than the national average.

Maryland Population 1950–2010

Baltimore, the largest city in Maryland, declined in population by more than 300,000 people between 1950 and 2010. During the same period, the state's population more than doubled. Based on the shift in the state economy toward services and employment by government, in what part of Maryland do you think much of the state's population growth took place?

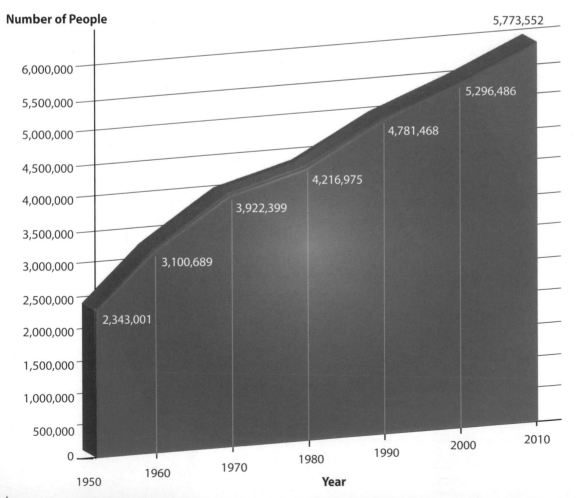

Number of People

- 5,773,552
- 5,296,486
- 4,781,468
- 4,216,975
- 3,922,399
- 3,100,689
- 2,343,001

Years: 1950, 1960, 1970, 1980, 1990, 2000, 2010

Year

Major hotels, shops, restaurants, and other attractions cluster around Baltimore's Inner Harbor area.

About four-fifths of Maryland's population lives along a strip of land that runs between Baltimore and Washington, D.C. Baltimore is Maryland's largest city as well as the center of most of its cultural and recreational activities. Dundalk is a large suburb of Baltimore.

Maryland also maintains a strong rural tradition, especially in the southern and western parts of the state. Smaller cities and towns in these areas enjoy many of the same conveniences as larger cities.

I DIDN'T KNOW THAT!

Silver Spring, College Park, and Bethesda are important residential suburbs located near Washington, D.C.

The Beltway is a major highway that crosses Maryland as it circles Washington, D.C. Many Maryland residents drive the Beltway each day as they commute to and from the nation's capital.

Maryland is densely populated, with more than 590 people per square mile of land area.

Susquehanna Indians were living in the Dundalk area when the first Europeans arrived. The modern history of Dundalk began in 1916 when the Bethlehem Steel company chose the area to build homes for shipyard workers. Dundalk took its name from a town in Ireland.

The capital of Maryland is Annapolis.
It was known in colonial times as the
"Athens of America" because of the
richness of its cultural and intellectual life.

Politics and Government

Maryland's government consists of three branches. The General Assembly, the state's legislative branch, passes the state's laws. The General Assembly has two chambers, or parts. They are a 47-member Senate and a 141-member House of Delegates. Members of both chambers are elected to four-year terms. Among the laws passed by the legislature was one in 1939 making "Maryland, My Maryland" the official state song. James Ryder Randall wrote the words to this song in April 1861, at the beginning of the Civil War. Randall wanted Maryland to side with the Confederacy, and he felt outrage when Union troops entered Baltimore.

The person responsible for carrying out the laws is the governor, who heads the state's executive branch and also serves a four-year term. Other elected members of the executive branch include the lieutenant governor, the attorney general, and the state **comptroller**.

The judicial branch is responsible for interpreting the state's laws. The state's highest court is the Court of Appeals.

Born in 1963, Martin O'Malley grew up in Bethesda and Rockville. He served as mayor of Baltimore before he became state governor in 2007.

Maryland's state song is called "Maryland, My Maryland."

Here is an excerpt from the song:

*The despot's heel is on thy shore,
Maryland!
His torch is at thy temple door,
Maryland!
Avenge the patriotic gore
That flecked the streets of Baltimore,
And be the battle queen of yore,
Maryland! My Maryland!*

*Hark to an exiled son's appeal,
Maryland!
My mother State! to thee I kneel,
Maryland!
For life and death, for woe and weal,
Thy peerless chivalry reveal,
And gird thy beauteous limbs with steel,
Maryland! My Maryland!*

Cultural Groups

Many Marylanders are of British or French **ancestry**. Settlers from other countries began arriving in the region in the 1700s. Germans settled near Frederick and then around Baltimore in the 1730s. Many Marylanders continue to celebrate traditional German customs and festivals, such as Oktoberfest.

Baltimore is a very diverse city, with people of many different national backgrounds. The largest groups include people of German, British, Irish, or Italian descent, and people of Polish, Czech, Greek, and Russian descent also live in the city. Neighborhoods throughout Baltimore help to preserve these distinctive European traditions.

In the 20th and early 21st centuries, Maryland received many immigrants from Asia and Latin America, adding to the state's cultural richness. One in ten Marylanders today was born outside the United States.

To serve its growing Latino population, Montgomery County offers health programs and other events that appeal to residents' Hispanic heritage.

During a visit to Baltimore, First Lady Michelle Obama spent time with inner-city students. She was promoting her "Let's Move" program to help children be fit and healthy.

African Americans are the state's largest minority group. Many African Americans in Maryland trace their ancestry from slaves who lived in the state. At the time of the first U.S. Census, slaves made up about one of every three state residents. After the Civil War, former slaves from the South moved north to Baltimore, where they joined a well-established community of blacks who had been free for several generations. Today, nearly two-thirds of Baltimore residents and about 30 percent of all Marylanders are African American.

Maryland has no federally recognized American Indian groups, and Indians make up less than 1 percent of the state's population. Maryland hosts several annual powwows and other cultural events that celebrate American Indian culture with traditional dancing, singing, crafts, and food. Yearly festivals include the Howard County Powwow and the American Indian Heritage Day Powwow in Silver Spring.

Arts and Entertainment

Maryland has produced many popular writers. Born in Baltimore in 1947, Tom Clancy published his first novel, *The Hunt for Red October*, in 1984. Like many of Clancy's later works, this "techno-thriller" blends suspense and modern technology with the world of politics. Many of Clancy's novels have been made into successful Hollywood films.

Another well-known Maryland novelist is Dashiell Hammett, who was born in St. Mary's County in 1894. His detective stories, such as *The Maltese Falcon* and *The Thin Man*, thrilled and captivated readers.

The journalist and critic H. L. Mencken, a native of Baltimore, also gained a national reputation. He wrote essays about literature and about what he considered the faults of American life. His book *The American Language*, first published in 1919, is considered a classic.

Marin Alsop, conductor of the Baltimore Symphony, was the first woman to serve as music director of a major U.S. orchestra.

Rolling Stone *magazine named Joan Jett one of the 100 greatest guitarists of all time.*

Maryland boasts many fine art museums, including the Baltimore Museum of Art. Founded in 1914, the museum is the largest in Maryland. Its collections include more than 85,000 objects from around the world and a library with about 50,000 books and magazines.

Classical music lovers in Maryland flock to the Joseph Meyerhoff Symphony Hall, home of the Baltimore Symphony Orchestra, and to the Lyric Opera House, also in Baltimore. The Maryland Hall for the Creative Arts, in Annapolis, showcases a variety of performing arts, including classical music, opera, and ballet.

Many nonclassical musicians have also called Maryland home. Billie Holiday is one of the most popular jazz musicians of all time. While she made her mark in New York City in the late 1920s, she never forgot her Baltimore home. Holiday's singing influenced musicians for decades to come, and her distinctive style was often imitated but rarely matched. Two more recent performers, Joan Jett and Tori Amos, grew up in Maryland.

The art collection of Baltimore's Walters Art Museum contains pieces from ancient Egypt to modern Europe.

Edgar Allan Poe, who wrote the poem "The Raven" and many scary stories, spent much of his adult life in Baltimore.

The Morris A. Mechanic Theater, in Baltimore, presents productions of touring Broadway shows.

Composer and guitarist Frank Zappa was born in Baltimore in 1940. He was inducted into the Rock and Roll Hall of Fame in 1995.

Film star Goldie Hawn grew up in Takoma Park. She has starred in *Cactus Flower*, *Private Benjamin*, *The First Wives Club*, *Death Becomes Her*, *Protocol*, *Foul Play*, and many other films.

Sports

Maryland residents and vacationers alike enjoy sailing, fishing, duck and goose hunting, skiing, and whitewater rafting. Calvert Cliffs is a popular spot for beachcombing, and the Appalachian Trail is good for hiking. With its long shoreline, Chesapeake Bay is a popular summer tourist attraction.

Jousting is an unusual sport that is popular with Marylanders. In modern jousting contests, competitors race their horses down an 80-yard track to spear three rings with their lances.

Horse racing is another popular Maryland pastime. The Preakness, held in Baltimore, is one of the most famous racing events in the country. It is one of the three horse races that make up the **Triple Crown**.

Lacrosse, played with a stick with a netted basket, is a fast-paced, exciting sport that is very popular in Maryland. The lacrosse teams from Johns Hopkins University and the University of Maryland are generally among the best in the country.

The Preakness regularly attracts the largest crowds of any Maryland sporting event. In 2010, nearly 100,000 people watched Lookin at Lucky race to victory.

In 3,001 regular-season games with the Baltimore Orioles, Cal Ripken, Jr., made 3,184 hits and blasted 431 home runs.

Maryland chose jousting as the state sport in 1962. Walking became the official state exercise in 2008.

Johnny Unitas starred at quarterback for the Baltimore Colts from 1956 through 1972. He helped lead the Colts to three league championships, including the Super Bowl in 1971.

The Lacrosse Museum and Lacrosse Hall of Fame are located at Johns Hopkins University in Baltimore.

Babe Ruth was born in Baltimore. Other Maryland-born baseball greats include Lefty Grove, Frank Baker, and Jimmie Foxx.

The state has several major professional sports teams. In Major League Baseball, the Baltimore Orioles play their games in the beautiful Oriole Park at Camden Yards. Oriole infielder Cal Ripken, Jr., captured the sporting world's attention with both his incredible talent and his endurance. From 1982 until 1998 he did not miss a game, setting a record of 2,632 consecutive games played. Ripken continued to wow fans with his hitting and fielding until his retirement after the 2001 season. He was inducted into the Baseball Hall of Fame in 2007.

In 1984, Maryland sports fans were crushed when the Baltimore Colts professional football team left Maryland for Indianapolis. The National Football League returned to the state in 1996 when the Baltimore Ravens played their first season. In 2001 the Ravens won the Super Bowl by beating the New York Giants, 34–7.

National Averages Comparison

The United States is a federal republic, consisting of fifty states and the District of Columbia. Alaska and Hawai'i are the only non-contiguous, or non-touching, states in the nation. Today, the United States of America is the third-largest country in the world in population. The United States Census Bureau takes a census, or count of all the people, every ten years. It also regularly collects other kinds of data about the population and the economy. How does Maryland compare to the national average?

Comparison Chart

United States 2010 Census Data *	USA	Maryland
Admission to Union	NA	April 28, 1788
Land Area (in square miles)	3,537,438.44	9,773.82
Population Total	308,745,538	5,773,552
Population Density (people per square mile)	87.28	590.72
Population Percentage Change (April 1, 2000, to April 1, 2010)	9.7%	9.0%
White Persons (percent)	72.4%	58.2%
Black Persons (percent)	12.6%	29.4%
American Indian and Alaska Native Persons (percent)	0.9%	0.4%
Asian Persons (percent)	4.8%	5.5%
Native Hawaiian and Other Pacific Islander Persons (percent)	0.2%	0.1%
Some Other Race (percent)	6.2%	3.6%
Persons Reporting Two or More Races (percent)	2.9%	2.9%
Persons of Hispanic or Latino Origin (percent)	16.3%	8.2%
Not of Hispanic or Latino Origin (percent)	83.7%	91.8%
Median Household Income	$52,029	$70,482
Percentage of People Age 25 or Over Who Have Graduated from High School	80.4%	83.8%

*All figures are based on the 2010 United States Census, with the exception of the last two items. Percentages may not add to 100 because of rounding.

How to Improve My Community

Strong communities make strong states. Think about what features are important in your community. What do you value? Education? Health? Forests? Safety? Beautiful spaces? Government works to help citizens create ideal living conditions that are fair to all by providing services in communities. Consider what changes you could make in your community. How would they improve your state as a whole? Using this concept web as a guide, write a report that outlines the features you think are most important in your community and what improvements could be made. A strong state needs strong communities.

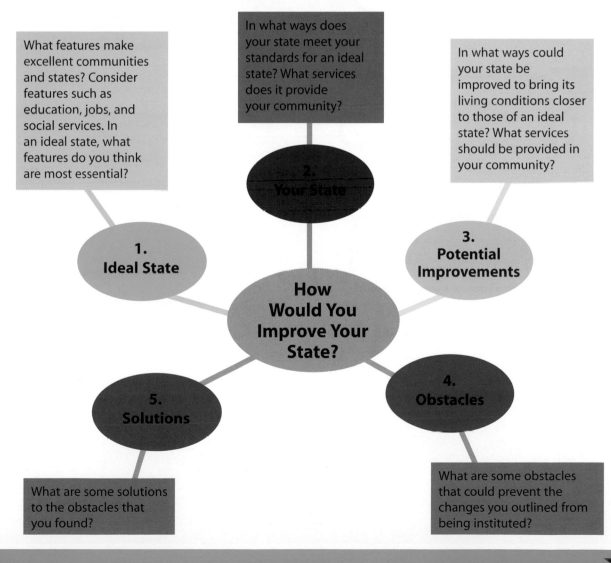

What features make excellent communities and states? Consider features such as education, jobs, and social services. In an ideal state, what features do you think are most essential?

In what ways does your state meet your standards for an ideal state? What services does it provide your community?

In what ways could your state be improved to bring its living conditions closer to those of an ideal state? What services should be provided in your community?

2.
Your State

1.
Ideal State

3.
Potential
Improvements

How
Would You
Improve Your
State?

5.
Solutions

4.
Obstacles

What are some solutions to the obstacles that you found?

What are some obstacles that could prevent the changes you outlined from being instituted?

Exercise Your Mind!

Think about these questions and then use your research skills to find the answers and learn more fascinating facts about Maryland. A teacher, librarian, or parent may be able to help you locate the best sources to use in your research.

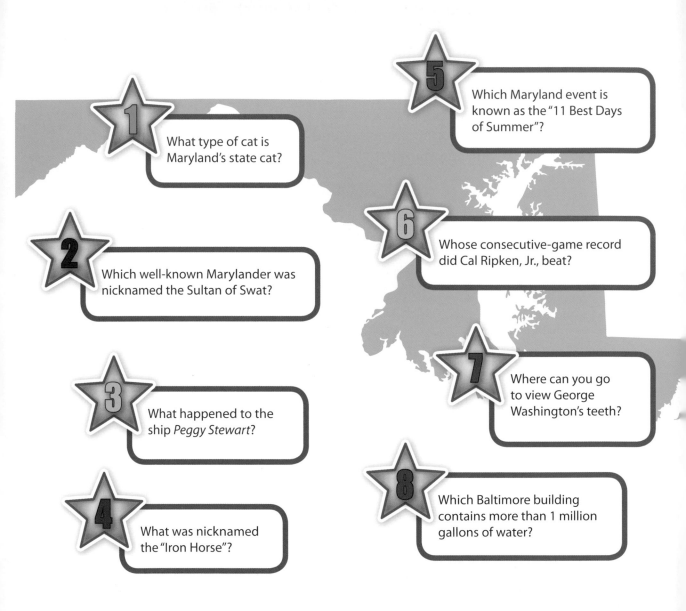

1 What type of cat is Maryland's state cat?

2 Which well-known Marylander was nicknamed the Sultan of Swat?

3 What happened to the ship *Peggy Stewart*?

4 What was nicknamed the "Iron Horse"?

5 Which Maryland event is known as the "11 Best Days of Summer"?

6 Whose consecutive-game record did Cal Ripken, Jr., beat?

7 Where can you go to view George Washington's teeth?

8 Which Baltimore building contains more than 1 million gallons of water?

Words to Know

ancestry: people from whom an individual or group is descended

broiler chickens: young chickens raised for meat rather than eggs

comptroller: official who reviews government income and spending

diversity: variety

endangered species: a kind of animal or plant that is in danger of completely dying out

estuary: the part of a river where it meets the sea, where fresh and salt water mix

hydroelectric: using waterpower to create electricity

nursery products: commercially grown plants

persecution: harsh treatment because of religious or political beliefs

plantation: a large estate that grows crops such as cotton, tea, and tobacco

textiles: fabrics made by weaving or knitting

Triple Crown: the title held by the horse that wins the Kentucky Derby, the Preakness, and the Belmont Stakes races

wetlands: swamps and marshes

Index

Log on to www.av2books.com

AV[2] by Weigl brings you media enhanced books that support active learning. Go to www.av2books.com, and enter the special code found on page 2 of this book. You will gain access to enriched and enhanced content that supplements and complements this book. Content includes video, audio, web links, quizzes, a slide show, and activities.

Audio
Listen to sections of the book read aloud.

Video
Watch informative video clips.

Embedded Weblinks
Gain additional information for research.

Try This!
Complete activities and hands-on experiments.

WHAT'S ONLINE?

Try This!	Embedded Weblinks	Video	EXTRA FEATURES
Test your knowledge of the state in a mapping activity.	Discover more attractions in Maryland.	Watch a video introduction to Maryland.	**Audio** Listen to sections of the book read aloud.
Find out more about precipitation in your city.	Learn more about the history of the state.	Watch a video about the features of the state.	**Key Words** Study vocabulary, and complete a matching word activity.
Plan what attractions you would like to visit in the state.	Learn the full lyrics of the state song.		
Learn more about the early natural resources of the state.			**Slide Show** View images and captions, and prepare a presentation.
Write a biography about a notable resident of Maryland.			
Complete an educational census activity.			**Quizzes** Test your knowledge.

AV[2] was built to bridge the gap between print and digital. We encourage you to tell us what you like and what you want to see in the future.

Sign up to be an AV[2] Ambassador at www.av2books.com/ambassador.